THE DILEMM.

The Dilemma

N.K. Aning

Published by N.K. Aning, 2021.

THE DILEMMA

First edition. July 18, 2021.

ISBN: 979-8201266172

Written by N.K. Aning.

Also by N.K. Aning

Imaginaterium
Pierce and the City of Imaginaterium
Pierce and the Fallen Gods
The legend of Pierce and Peter : The Dawn

Poetry
In Her Eyes
The Agony of Life
A Memory of Death

Short Stories
The Bronze Man's Secret
Jack and God
Jason And The Great Dragon
The State
First Contact
The Agony of a Slave

Watch for more at https://www.facebook.com/N-K-Aning-879564645456623/.

Table of Contents

To those who are not afraid to question.

PART ONE
THE GOD DILEMMA

"All you really need to know for the moment is that the universe is a lot more complicated than you might think, even if you start from a position of thinking it's pretty damn complicated in the first place."
Adams Douglas

Acknowledgements

Grateful acknowledgement is given to the following personalities for the beautiful quotes in this book: John Milton, Isaac Newton, Immanuel Kant, Jeremy Taylor, Ernest Hemingway, and Albert Einstein. All scripture quotations are from the New King James Version.

Introduction

As a child, I had access to a ton of books from my dad. I remember my dad bringing a boxload of novels home one day. My curiosity was piqued as I read through all those books one by one. I used to enjoy staring at artistic renderings of biblical stories. There was this little book about prehistoric animals I was fascinated with. The book showed different stages of evolution, archeologist attempting to carbon date dinosaur bones. I was thrilled to read about these giant creatures. I recall reading about prehistoric men. There was this nagging question at the back of my head, but of course, being from a religious family, I couldn't ask these questions. I often wondered to myself, if these stories of prehistoric men were true, then what did it mean for the biblical story of Adam and Eve? It is in this respect that I set out to examine some of the themes of the natural world and religion. I am no expert on science or religion. Therefore, I ask this question; what would a lay person think of the many controversial themes in the bible?

Chapter One
Creation

"This most beautiful system of the sun, planets and comets, could only proceed from the counsel and dominion of an intelligent and powerful Being." Isaac Newton.

These are the words of an influential scientist in his time. The creation story is one that many great thinkers have grappled with over the centuries. The bible states that "In the beginning when God created the universe.." This statement clearly shows that creation was initiated by an intelligent being. The first humans, Adam and Eve were created by God and from them all mankind was spawned. As a lay person I don't have enough evidence or proof to suggest otherwise.

Creation according to some evolutionist began through the big bang. How exactly this happened is still a subject of contention? Evolution is a fascinating theory yet the great question still remains. What could have caused the big bang? How did a single unprecedented event lead to life as we know it? Even Charles Darwin admitted the difficulty with his theory, if I am not wrong.

Back to the main question. As a lay person who is neither an expert in theology or evolution, my question is this; what would common sense dictate? Is it reasonable to assume that such a complex and beautiful universe could have sprung up by chance? Was creation by accident or design?

The answer to this question lies in part in our social conditioning. No one can deny that the family we are born into help shapes our beliefs about life. I recall fondly as a child reading a book on fossils. These giant creatures had gone extinct while two-footed creatures like us had lived on. As I read these books on prehistoric men, I asked myself if God had created Adam and Eve, what about the Neanderthals? Was it an elaborate hoax by some scientist to discredit the biblical story of creation? Judging from the millions of humans on this planet, is it reasonable to assume that Adam and Eve were the first humans? Is it also reasonable to assume that the existence of life on earth was the result of a single improbable event like the big bang?

To the evolutionist, it would be preposterous to assume that creation originated from an intelligent being. But to the lay person, neither science nor religion adequately addresses the question of creation sufficiently enough. There are still many unanswered questions. Evolution might not offer a better explanation to the complexities of life, but it doesn't negate the fact that religion, Christianity for that matter hasn't also done enough to sate the curiosity of the lay person. To a lay person creation by design would be more preferable as the words of Jeremy Taylor succinctly puts:

"What can be more foolish than to think that all this rare fabric of heaven and earth could come by chance, when all the skills of science is not able to make an oyster."

Chapter Two
God

The name "God" is perhaps the most researched subject in the history of literature. The presence and the existence of God has sparked countless debates, articles and essays from eminent personalities such as Richard Dawkins and John Lennox. In some cultures, He is referred to as "The Supreme Being". But for the purposes of this write up, I would stick to the biblical definition of God. In this context, he is the creator of the universe according to biblical traditions.

Now, if a lay person never having the benefit of studying the bible was approached and told his or her existence was because of a supreme being, what would be that individual's response?

To a logical and critical thinker, the concept of an All-knowing, Omnipresent and All-powerful deity is a bit problematic. The idea of being accountable and beholden to an All-powerful deity while the dream of a Christian, does not sit so well with an atheist or non believers.

To a large extent, most atheists believe everything must have a cause. Having an uncreated creator behind the creation of the universe is a bit problematic for some people. So the question we must ask is this; Is God, the force behind the design of the universe or just an imaginary being who we fear will punish us if we don't become subservient to him?

In many debates, the concept of God is defended by theist is that 'God exists, but this cannot be proven or disproven.'

The difficulty in believing in any creator of any kind is the question of suffering. God as the many epithets implies, is All-knowing, and All-powerful yet cannot stop the suffering of this world. That is the question most atheists ask of a seemingly benevolent being.

The concept of God while not covered extensively here presents another question. If God is all powerful, then why did such an All-powerful being allow suffering to happen in the first place? Albert

Einstein succinctly stated "*I cannot believe that God would choose to play dice with the universe.*"

Chapter Three
The Question of Evil

"The mind is its own place, and in itself can make a heaven of hell, a hell of heaven..." John Milton, Paradise lost.

A son shot his mother..

A terrorist blew himself up..

A teenager shot a group..

The above are the headlines you hear every day, over the years. Evil is real and rampant in our ever changing world. From robberies, murder and rape, to mention a few, the list goes on. At the centre of these atrocities is the question of where evil originated from. To a lay person, how can an All-powerful God sit by idly as pain and suffering happen under his omniscient gaze.

Fortunately for us the Bible has an answer to that, albeit one that does not satisfy its critics. The source of evil is blamed on a celestial being, Lucifer.

Christians would argue that the suffering of the patriarch Job was not brought by God, yet the Creator could have prevented the devil from raining down calamity upon Job in the first place. He actually gave the devil permission. Does God support evil then?

In the print and electronic media, we learn of children being raped, children dying of cancer and other equally horrendous diseases. I once read a comment on a BBC page where someone asked why a loving God would give cancer to a five year old? These are not easy questions to answer. Pain is real. People die; they go through so much hardship. Is it enough to accept the answer that all this evil happens because Adam and Eve ate from a forbidden tree? Why would an All-knowing God create a couple, gift them with dominion over everything and command them not to eat from a tree planted right under their noses? Is the eating of the forbidden fruit a literal interpretation or is there something more to it?

Either way it does not truly satisfy the question of the origin of evil. Is it also right to blame the devil, imaginary or not for the morally wrong deeds we do?

One man sits at his dinner table and says "I thank God for saving my family from the accident." another family weeps over their loss. Who should they thank? The devil?

Is it not enough to wake up everyday bombarded with all sorts of violence and abuse in this morally corrupt world? The constant stream of violence towards women and children? As C. S Lewis put it, "There is no neutral ground in the universe. Every square inch, every split second, is claimed by God and counterclaimed by the devil."

What would be more preposterous than this statement to an atheist or a non-believer. Are the lives of mortals so insignificant as to play dice with?

Yet this is the nature of suffering in this world. If God created Lucifer, then by implication He allowed suffering to thrive. Of course, any Christian would dispute that statement. Perchance the Bible would provide some enlightenment on that.

Chapter Four
The Bible

"I believe that the existence of the Bible is the greatest benefit to the human race. Any attempt to belittle it, I believe, is a crime against humanity." Immanuel Kant

The Bible is without doubt the single most read and widely distributed book in the history of literature. No book has churned so many countless essays, quotes, commentaries and debates in history. The Bible has survived centuries of rigorous analysis.

But what makes the Bible so special? The bible is a compilation of different writings over a span of many years. It entails stories of the creation of man, redemption of God's chosen nation. It is a book peppered with the wisdom of the ages. It chronicles the journey of the Israelites from Egypt and finally settling down in Canaan.

If one is not told that the Bible is a divinely inspired work, it would be a great literary epic. Despite the poetic words, miracles and stories of redemption, there is a subtle hint of two personalities of God running through the Bible. This brings us to the nature of God.

Chapter Five
The Nature of God

"And fear not them which kill the body, but are not able to kill the soul. But rather fear him which is able to destroy both soul and body in hell."

The Christian God is seen as a loving, compassionate and forgiving deity in the new testament. But the picture is quite different when one takes a critical look at the old testament. There we see a different kind of God, one that is vindictive, jealous and vengeful. Yet to the ordinary Christian such an outlook on God is contradictory to their beliefs of a loving God.

By studying the scriptures, any lay person would be surprised by the subtle but palpable change in God. While the new testament portrays God as long suffering, this is not so in the old testament. What could account for this?

"Recompense to no man evil for evil. Provide things honest in the sight of all men" Romans 12:37. This statement is far different from the God of the old testament. This can be evidenced from the flood wiping out almost the entire human race. In modern terms, that would be called genocide. But of course, when God does it, He is simply eliminating sin from the earth.

As a child I was delighted when I had a copy of the book of Bible stories. It had these beautiful illustrations of important moments from the Bible. One of these illustrations was the wall of Jericho. For any Christian, the miraculous crumbling of the wall of Jericho was a divine feat. But there is an ugly truth any lay person would immediately deduce. Jericho, I am no historian, but I am pretty sure it was a bustling city full of a gamut of individual, from the everyday trader, to the little children scurrying around the streets, up to no good. These were mortals carrying on their normal lives. A whole city was crushed to death in a gruesome way to the very last person, even the unborn children were not spared. God allowed such an atrocity. Why?

Why does a seemingly vengeful deity in the old testament metamorphosize into a loving God in the new testament? That is the million dollar question.

Throughout the old testament, a nagging question keeps running through. Why would a benevolent God ask men to do such horrible things? Yet it is a common theme throughout the old testament. Is this consistent with the nature of God as seen in the new testament?

The afflictions of Job, the flood and the crumbling of the wall of Jericho, condemning innocent lives for the sins of their fathers. These are but a few of the many things difficult to grasp in the Bible. Any lay person would question the seemingly inconsistent thread on the nature of God. Another controversial topic is the concept of hell.

Chapter Six

Hell

"The bodies of the damned shall be crowded together in hell, like grapes in a winepress, which press on one another till they burst, every distinct sense and organ shall be assailed with its own appropriate and most exquisite sufferings." Jeremy Taylor

"You will go to hell if you don't come to church." The Sunday school teacher would say to wide-eyed children. These were the words spoken to little children about the concept of hell. Hell was described as a place of perpetual torment. While there are many varying descriptions of hell, one thing is certain, no one would dream of being there. Again, any lay person would ask, why would a loving God condemn any human to such an abominable place?

Centuries past, the word 'hell' was such a distressing word, the mere threat of it made unsuspecting church members agonize in fear. Some were willing to pay any amount just to avoid that horrible place. Duplicity of course, it only enriched the clergy.

But why is the subject of hell, so crucial to Christianity?

Hell, according to the Bible was created for the devil and his angels. Yet the distress that the subject of hell causes among folks causes some men of God not to talk about it. Yet it is a divisive subject in the modern day church. Some believe there is no hell; rather the unsaved would cease to exist. It is the second school of thought we are much interested in. Is it justifiable to condemn a human being to an eternity of torment?

Some would argue that for the likes of Adolf Hitler, it is justifiable. But what about children, infants not baptized? Let's make it simple, from a lay person's view, you either belong to God or you find yourself in hell.

So the question remains; what about the bushmen who have lived their entire lives devoid of any contact with Christian missionaries? Are they bound for hell since they are not believers? It is a horrible imagery to conjure. Yet that is the fate of every individual that does not believe in God according to Christianity. Unless there is a grand plan of redemption we are not aware of. No sane human being would want to wish hell upon anyone, no matter their crimes. That being said, the concept of hell is one that still divides the Christian faith, but for any lay person it is a hard truth to digest.

Conclusion

"A man may be a heretic in the truth, and if he believes things only because his pastor says so, or the assembly so determines, without knowing other reason, though his belief be true, yet the very truth he holds becomes his heresy." John Milton

Religion can either be a curse or a blessing to mankind. It depends on how we see it. Countless wars, atrocities have been committed in the name of religion, Christianity not excluded. If the story of Moses is to be believed, I am in no way stating that it isn't- the killing of the firstborn sons of Egypt was an abominable thing to do. The persecution of individuals and families by the church, suppression of truth and hindering scientific progress has dented the image of the church over the centuries. Religion, Christianity to be precise, has been propagated in almost every country on this planet. Yet why has a religion committed to love failed continuously to put an end to countless pain, grief and atrocities committed?

Despite the failings of Christianity, we cannot be ignorant of the fact that it has also done a lot to improve the lives of many people. I dare not say that the Christianity practiced today is a perfect reflection of what the gospels preached. There are still many unanswered questions about the origins of humanity and religion. No book provides the full answers. Perchance, one day science together with religion might show us the way. For if all we aspire to be after death is a bunch of atoms, then that is a miserable existence indeed. While I cannot deny that the idea of eternal bliss does sound appealing even to the intellectually enlightened, as a lay person, standing under the vast skies, observing the starry heavens, how can one not wonder how perfectly designed this universe is? In the end only death would truly show us what lies ahead.

Ernest Hemingway succinctly put it, *"Every man's life ends the same way. It is only the details of how he lived and how he died that distinguish one man from the other."*

16

PART TWO
THE CHRISTIAN DILEMMA

Chapter One

The Creation of Adam and Eve

From an early age, we are taught how Adam and Eve were the first humans created in a beautiful and lush garden, the Garden of Eden, a perfect place for the two couples created by God. As a child, it was a fantastic tale. But growing up, reading other books, getting to know about the prehistoric world, one wonders if indeed the biblical Adam and Eve were the progenitors of the human race as we know it. While I must admit that there are similar stories of creation in other myths and legends that echoes that of the Christian religion, the creation account in the bible is by far the most popular.

Were Adam and Eve really the beginning of the human race?

What about outside the Garden of Eden? If there were no humans outside, then who did Cain marry and how did he build his city? An even more interesting aspect of the first humans was their life span. It is unthinkable that they could age up to almost a thousand years.

Considering the evidence of fossil records and archeological discoveries made within the last century, can we really vouch for the story of Adam and Eve?

Scientist claim the first humans evolved some millions of years ago? But can we really trust their words when discoveries are made to contradict their claims.

Is Adam then the truly first human? What about Eve being created from the rib of Adam as the bible clearly states? While some schools of thought believe God created Adam and Eve in his image, others believe Eve was created after Adam. This interpretation invariably has led to the marginalization and subjugation of women over the centuries.

But the central question still remains. Despite the centuries of research into the origins of humanity, our beginning still remains a mystery. Were Adam and Eve the first humans of the creation story or was it just an allegory to explain the existence of mankind? Either way, it is a very controversial and difficult question to answer and that leads us to the next question.

Chapter Two

The Tree of the Knowledge of Good and Evil

"But of the fruit of the tree which is in the midst of the garden, God hath said, Ye shall not eat of it, neither shall ye touch it, lest ye die."

This was the commandment given by the biblical God to Adam and Eve after they were created and placed in the Garden of Eden. Such a simple command, right? But curiosity got the better of Eve and she did eat from the forbidden tree, forever dooming humanity to the seeds of corruption. But let's pause there for a moment. Why create a garden, fill it with all manner of beautiful trees and animals and then plant a forbidden tree in it? Interesting question, isn't it?

On the face of it, as Christians we are taught to believe that Eve eating from the forbidden tree brought sin into the world. But here is the question, why did God plant that tree in the first place knowing fully well that Eve would eat of the tree anyway? Kind of like asking a child not to take a chocolate placed in front of him knowing very well he is going to eat it anyway. Why place it there in the first place? Why let the first humans go through a test they would fail anyway? What's the essence?

In effect the biblical God knew the first humans would rebel anyway regardless of the commands he gave them. Yet the idea of their rebellion was not instigated by them but a celestial being serving under God. Yet they took the brunt of the punishment. Who was this celestial being who doomed humanity to the wrath of God?

Chapter Three
Lucifer Morningstar

Lucifer Morningstar, light bringer, the adversary, these and many more identify the famous archangel in Christian lore. Due to movies, books and music, the name Lucifer has gained notoriety as the adversary of God. His name is associated with everything unholy. With television shows either vilifying him or praising him, Lucifer has become a part of our history.

According to the bible, Lucifer in the guise of a serpent was the one who deceived Eve in the Garden of Eden. While some believe this assertion, others in Christendom reject this assertion. But who was Lucifer?

According to biblical history, Lucifer was an angel of the Lord. The bible seems to suggest he was a Cherub, a guardian of the throne of God.

Yet an interesting hypothesis comes up, if heaven, the dwelling place of God was a perfect place, how could Lucifer, a perfect being rebel against God? It presupposes God being perfect and almighty would have fore knowledge of the rebellion of Lucifer. Yet here we have Lucifer, an archangel, under the all-powerful creator leading a third of the host of heaven in rebellion against the creator himself. It raises a lot of questions, doesn't it?

Some schools of thought posit that Lucifer was expelled from the celestial city because of his pride, he sought to over throw God. In human terms, dictators are overthrown. Was that the case? Were some angels dissatisfied with the reign of the creator? This is just speculation of course. Another school of thought teaches that Lucifer failed to bow down to man when God commanded it. Though this is not biblical, a lot of people do believe this assertion from other books.

But the obvious question many Christians grapple with is this; If God is all-powerful, why didn't he stop Lucifer? This is a difficult question to answer. Throughout the bible, Lucifer is portrayed to be the adversary of God. Why did God allow Lucifer to tempt Eve? These are the questions many Christians have and yet cannot ask in church for fear of being ridiculed or worse they are not given satisfactory answers.

If indeed the story of Lucifer is to be believed, then it means centuries of war, diseases, slavery, have all emanated from that one single act of rebellion by a celestial being against his creator, yet an all-powerful God failed to stop him. This raises a further conundrum about the immutable attributes of God.

Chapter Four
The Three Immutable Attributes of God

As a child, I used to recite the three famous attributes of God; Omnipresent, Omnipotent and Omniscient. Translated as God is everywhere, all-powerful and all-knowing. Yet whenever the rebellion of Lucifer comes up, wouldn't an all-powerful God have been able to stop Lucifer in the first place.

In addition, an omniscient God would have known beforehand that creating Lucifer would bring untold repercussions on our world unless of course there was a cosmic grand design we are yet to comprehend with our mortal minds. But alas the question of free will pops up. But a nagging question still remains, if indeed Lucifer had freewill, then it presupposes that the choice of Lucifer was not etched in stone, it could have been prevented. This would mean that the choice of Lucifer precipitated the fall of mankind.

If indeed he had freewill, then the future was unknown but then an omniscient God would have foreknowledge of the choice Lucifer, Adam and Eve, and even the choices of the entire human race. That is a scary thought. Is there really free will then? God already knew the action he would take even before Lucifer had rebelled. That creates a series of contradictions no one can answer. Maybe it's just a fantasy but God being all powerful could have just snapped his hand and all this untold suffering and death could have been avoided. Yet this is not so, why?

Mankind is punished for the sins of others. For instance, when the angels deserted their places in heaven and consorted with mortal women, God being Omniscient should have known, right? Yet we have the whole human race wiped out because of the transgressions of a few angels. Time after time we witness the wrath and vengeance of God against powerless mortals. Interestingly, we have a very different outlook of God in the New Testament.

Chapter Five

The God of the Old Testament and the God of the New Testament

A careful reading through the Old Testament reveals a very interesting side of God from that of the God of the New Testament. As a child it was fun to read the book of bible stories with all the fantastic imagery of the stories depicted in its pages. But to tell the truth, it would take a truly heartless person not to wince at some of the atrocities committed in the name of God. Take the wall of Jericho, a whole city crumbled to dust, men, women, children, pregnant women and even animals perished. God instructing Saul to eliminate all his enemies, in our generation it would have been called genocide. But we may make a justification that it was a time of war. But time after time we find the God of the Old Testament venting his wrath upon mankind. From the destruction of entire cities, to the tower of Babel because apparently mankind was becoming too powerful, these are the sides of the Old Testament God.

Some schools of thought posit that during the time of the Old Testament, God was closer to mankind and hence there was a need for stiffer punishments for their disobedience. But interestingly in the New Testament, there is a radical transformation in the God we know. It is no longer about eliminating your enemies but turning the other cheek. Such a radical shift might go unnoticed, but to some Christians it is a bit jarring for them. How do they explain the sudden change? An argument was proposed that humanity was sinful. What about the story of Job? Was he a sinful man, yet we have the almighty creator placing a wager on the life of a mortal.

The killing of the firstborns of the Egyptians is an even more interesting event. How do we justify a loving creator punishing the Pharaoh by killing innocent children who had done nothing against God? Their only sin was that they were Egyptians caught up in a feud between God and the Pharaoh. Another instance, we have the God of the Old Testament wiping out an entire human race, the few survivors escaping in an ark. If indeed the story of the flood is to be believed, then all life on earth was destroyed through the great deluge. What an awful way to die. Couldn't an all-powerful God come up with a more inventive way to eliminate humans? But it begs the question, why flood the planet in forty days when you could have done it in one day? Interesting, isn't it? Yet the story of the flood is echoed in so many myths and legends, what are we missing?

These are but a few of the events perpetuated by the Old Testament God and yet he transforms into a loving, merciful and long suffering God in the New Testament. What happened? Why the sudden change? A very difficult question to answer. Yet while the New Testament portrays God as a loving one, there is still the matter of hell to consider. Why would a loving God condemn anyone to an eternity of suffering and punishment?

Chapter Six
Does Hell Exist?

"You will go to hell if you don't be a good boy or good girl."

Well, you hear that a lot from pastors and parents to their wards. Hell, a topic so controversial that some pastors shy away from it for fear of losing church members. But this is the dilemma of many Christians, the belief that the rejection of God means an eternity in hell fire.

Just the mention of hell evokes feelings of fear and horrible imaginations of torture by demons with pitchforks. This has been further exacerbated by modern literature and television shows.

But the question still remains, is hell a real place and why would a loving God create such a horrible place? Yes, the bible says it was created for the devil and his angels. Yet the idea that a human soul would be damned into hell for eternity is unthinkable. No human would want to wish such a thing unto his or her worst enemy.

Interestingly, Christendom seems to differ on this controversial topic. While some do not out rightly believe in hell of any kind, others do and are cautious in talking about it. There are those who spend their lives threatening people about going to hell. The bible does not specifically state what exactly happens there, but different interpretations of hell have been given by various scholars. Most are unaware they make their inferences from the literature of Dante. The church has been heavily influenced by his works albeit unknowingly. Yet given a choice between hell and oblivion, am sure a lot of people would opt for the latter.

How does a loving God condemn his own creation to an eternity in hell? Many Christians ponder about this question but are afraid to voice it. If indeed the doctrine of hell is to be believed, then judging from the current state of the world, then millions are destined for that infernal place. The imagery of such a thought is a horrible one to behold. But can we trust that the writers of the bible had this in mind when penning down the biblical text? That is our next question to ponder about.

Chapter Seven

Can We Trust The Bible As The Absolute Truth?

The bible is by far the bestselling book of all time. It is not without its controversies but the question really is this; can we really trust the bible as a genuine historical manuscript?

It is without doubt one of the most inspirational book ever written by mankind yet it has its errors and controversies like any other book. Can we trust the accounts in them as truth or fiction?

It is interesting to note that some of the stories are without doubt echoes of stories in other myths and legends but it does not detract from the originality of the scriptures. Researchers are still grappling with questions such as if some of the people portrayed in the bible really existed or not. The central figure of Christianity, Jesus Christ, is still being debated in certain quarters as to whether he truly existed or not and that is what truly makes the bible a truly remarkable book in our time.

Despite the many controversies surrounding the bible, it still remains a powerful book in our century. Scores of researchers have combed through the bible to discredit it and yet have made compelling case for its authenticity. Many atheists have converted after doing a rigorous analysis of its subject. Nations have been founded upon the principles of the bible. It is without doubt a very useful book in our generation but it has its flaws due to the time period it was written in.

There are many stories in it that would be frowned upon in today's world. Stories of genocide, slavery, incest, racial prejudice, discrimination, to mention a few, characterize some events in the bible. The bible is not a perfect book yet it remains a powerful book in our century.

Chapter Eight
Is Tongue Speaking Of Today Real?

The day of Pentecost is a major event in the Christian calendar. It was a day that the followers of Jesus in a room upstairs, after being filled with the spirit, spoke in tongues. According to the bible, the apostles spoke in the native tongues of the people at the time. They prophesied and spoke in different tongues.

Yet it is curious that the tongues of today are vastly different from that of the ones the apostles spoke after the death of Jesus. An ignorant person, upon entering a Pentecostal or charismatic church, during a prayer session might be tempted to say that the church members have been afflicted by a disease when he or she is bombarded by the apparent "unintelligible sounds" if one did not know better. But those are not just noises but the tongues of the spirit, participants are in direct communion with God.

I do not make a mockery of tongue speaking. There are many mysteries of Christianity which surpasses human understanding. But there is a divide in the church with regards to tongue speaking of today. While some claim that today's tongue speaking is real, others doubt this assertion. Either way, I cannot prove or discount such claims, in the end it is a mystery left only to the creator himself.

Chapter Nine
Is Tithing For Real?

Tithing is a major tenet of many churches in today's world. This practice originated from the Old Testament. Some bible scholars trace it back to the time of Abraham when he paid a tithe to the king of Salem, Melchizedek, after winning a great battle. Yet the question of tithing is still a very poignant and divisive topic in our church today.

Some Christians believe paying tithes was for the dispensation under the Old Testament. Hence under the New Testament, they are not required to pay any tithes. Those who advocate for it use Malachi subtly to enforce compliance of it. But the question really is this; is tithing really for our generation? Will you be cursed because you do not pay your tithes?

What about the countless Christians whose faith doesn't require them to pay tithes? Are they losing out because they are not adhering to the tithe paying principle? These are the questions young people ask and they do not get satisfactory answers. It is without doubt that the church needs money to run its operations. There is nothing wrong with paying tithe so long as they are paying not out of fear or compulsion but of their own free will.

Chapter Ten
What Would Jesus Do?

It is strange to note that despite the many churches and messages preached across the length and breadth of this world, the world is still in a sorry state. Sometimes, it is mind boggling just listening to news happening across the world. For a religion that preaches love, it lacks a lot. I stand to be corrected but I believe close to half the populations of this world are Christians and yet we do not see the world better off.

The central tenet of the gospel of Jesus was to love one another. Yet even in our churches, members are rife with jealousy, hatred, self-aggrandizement, racial prejudice, to mention a few. Is this what Jesus would have wanted? From millionaire televangelists who promise you God's blessing in return for your every penny, pastors who sexually abuse their church members, religious leaders living exorbitant lifestyles yet their member live impoverished lives. This is the church we find ourselves in, a church which rakes in millions but does little for the world.

Would Jesus be proud of the flock today? We have people starving and suffering yet we are concerned about erecting magnificent cathedrals, getting more donations to line our pockets, buying more private jets. I believe there are many Christians with so many questions on the sorry state of the church yet cannot ask for fear of being sidelined.

In the end, after all the doctrines, the money and the lust for fame or approval, only one poignant message of Jesus remains, "Love one another." This is a faith that promises so much but delivers very little and this, my friends, is the dilemma we face as Christians.

PART THREE

GOD IN THE MIDST OF PAIN AND SUFFERING

The Will of God

Imagine this scene, two children sitting in a sofa, sobbing uncontrollably as they stare at the dead body of their mother. A pastor has been called to comfort them. After eulogizing the dead person, the man of God ends his words by saying, "It is the will of God."

The children are young so they may not understand the enormity of what the man of God has said. If they are lucky, they might get some relatives to take care of them. If not they will go through life with all the misery and pain of losing their loved one. Yet this is the crux of the matter, "it is the Will of God."

But how can death, pain, depression be the will of God? Countless people die in road accidents, from sickness and yet we say it is the will of God, why? Why would a loving creator willingly condemn His creation to such untold suffering all just because everything is subjected to His will?

Is it fair for children to be orphaned because God wills it?

Is it fair for children to get cancer?

Is it fair for a little child in the Middle East to constantly fear for his or her life just because some sniper might shoot her at any time?

What is indeed the will of God?

As a Christian, you get the sense that people believe that everything that happens is the will of God. Yet it is simply unthinkable that the untold pain and suffering happening to humanity is the sovereign will of God.

It is downright insulting for some well-meaning individual to suggest to people going through pain or suffering that it is the will of God.

Is it the will of God that we should wallow in pain? Does God glorify himself in pain? Was it the will of God for countless people to be tortured and killed, children raped? How can we justify such atrocities by simply stating it is the will of God?

How can the will of God be cruel to humanity or is there something we are failing to understand?

Is God Selective?

I once watched a video of a child who was nearly run over by a truck and yet somehow miraculously escaped death. It was curious how a lot of the people commenting on the event said it was due to the goodness of God. How come the goodness of God didn't extend to the little girl in India raped by men? What about the children starving in Yemen? Where was the goodness of God?

Is God selective then?

The statements made by Christians on a daily basis seems to suggest it. Apparently He chooses to save a child from being hit by a truck but He is unable to save a child in Pakistan from a bomb.

Why does it seem that God in his infinite wisdom chooses to save some and not others? How does one family get to thank God for a full meal and yet at the same time another is starving to death? How do we justify the goodness of God in the face of such insurmountable pain and suffering? Does God not hear the cries of the oppressed in India, the starving in Yemen, the displaced in Myanmar? Why do some people seem to have it all and others facing such odds? Yet there is no discernable difference in their dedication to their creator.

Why does it seem that God is selective when it comes to humanity?

God Will Provide

There is nothing more annoying than the statement 'God will provide' made by some people just to provide an excuse for their inaction.

It is even more strange when leaders are supposed to act, they resort to long prayers and calling upon God to provide a way. What is even astounding is during the Covid-19 pandemic when scientist were busily researching for a vaccine, others were praying to God to put an end to it. Was God not there in the first place when the pandemic happened? I am not making a mockery of the consequences of the pandemic but it is simply astounding that people fail to see reason when they think God will provide. I am not suggesting that we do without God but isn't it curious that God who is omniscient gazed on as the pandemic scoured through every continent and yet we somehow hope He will provide an answer to that.

I believe the human mind has the intellect to solve problems generated by ourselves.

What is the essence of a creator providing for us when we have the tools to do that?

The statement 'God will provide' will simply not suffice to lift us out of our pain and suffering. Humans have gone through countless pain and suffering and it was by ingenuity and putting our God given brain to task that has elevated us to where we are today but not by simply saying words which have no meaning for human suffering.

"God will provide" will simply not do anything for humanity when faced with untold pain and suffering.

Cruelty of Mankind and the Grace of God

The single most powerful tool of wickedness is the human mind. From the Nazi concentration camps to the suicide bombings in the Middle East, countless humans have suffered under the onslaught of human wickedness. Innocents have been killed in the name of God. Women, children have suffered untold miseries just because of the ambition of a few. Yet whenever we question this wickedness we are told it is just by the Grace of God that He allows it.

Sometimes when you listen to the news, it's unthinkable that fellow human beings are willing to inflict such pain and suffering on each other. Yet the bigger question is, 'Where is God in all this?'

How does a loving creator standby while all this happens under his watchful gaze?

While others thank God for their meal, another starves in a different place. Innocent children, pregnant women are targeted by suicide bombers, why?

We pray for the grace of God and yet the outside world suffers, groaning under the pain of suffering. It is not enough to offer sympathy when the people don't see their God in whom they have faith not acting. How can God love his children and yet watch aloof as they experience such pain and suffering?

When will it end?

Origin of All Suffering and Pain

We live in a fallen world. This statement is known to almost every Christian. As the good book says, God created a perfect system yet it was corrupted by an angel, Lucifer. All human pain and suffering stem from one single act of Lucifer deceiving Eve and damming the entire human race. Strange that ever since then women have been subjugated and discriminated against because "Eve ate the forbidden fruit." Yet we have a creator omniscient and all powerful who failed to stop a rebellion in his kingdom and humans paid the price. Sounds a bit harsh but is that not the case? But if God had stopped Lucifer, then all this pain and suffering could have been averted or maybe not. Yet God doesn't do that but banishes the human race from the Garden of Eden into the world of pain and suffering and effectively makes the woman a slave to the man for all time.

But who dares question God?

After all He has a grand plan in place.

One that will see all human suffering come to an end in heaven. For those that refuse to kneel to him will be damned to hell to experience pain and suffering for all eternity.

Conclusion

Pain and suffering will not end while we live here on this mortal plane. As unthinkable as we can imagine, there are some things we cannot rely on God to aid us in. That is not to say that we don't need the creator but He simply cannot alleviate our pain and suffering for us while we live our days on this earth.

Wouldn't it be a sight for the creator to snap his fingers and all suffering ended but that is a fantasy we cannot entertain.

Is it the will of God that we suffer, I believe not but such is the nature of human life? No matter how much we abhor it, suffering is bound to happen in one form or another.

We can only hope that God will grant us the fortitude to stand in the midst of pain and suffering.

PART FOUR
REALITY

CREATION

What is the origin of humanity? Where do we come from? This simple yet complex question has hounded many people for centuries. There are some who believe in a creator notable amongst them Christians. The simple explanation according to them was that the universe was brought into existence by a creator. There are some on the other side who believe that life as we know it emerged from a phenomenon known as the Big Bang. While both theories might be simple to explain, they inadvertently complicate matters further. There are some who even subscribe to the notion of seeding by extraterrestrial entities from space even though such theories are unreasonable and quite extreme. The simple truth is that we do not really know our origins as humanity.

Now, granted that creation came about through the Big Bang. Then what is the ultimate purpose of life? There would be no purpose to such a random event unless it was guided yet that is not what the Big Bang is about. Is existence meaningless then if we are just a bunch of atoms from a random cosmic explosion of matter? That would be a bleak existence indeed. While there are many proponents of these theories, prominent among them Richard Dawkins, there is still the complicated matter of what caused the Big Bang in the first place. This is something we have not gotten an answer to despite several theories and research undertaken on it. If for a moment we were to believe in the Big Bang, then it means as a species we evolved from lower animals. What is the purpose of reality then? The Big Bang and evolution might be a popular creation theory yet it still doesn't offer us enough answers.

Now let's consider creation as the deist would have us believe. The creation story in this context while a simple one has it own problems. Who is this intelligent being who would create humanity and leave us to our own devices? What is the purpose of our creation? Are we serving some higher purpose while still on this planet? The reality of the matter is that we do not really have answers to these questions. There are countless religions on these planets. Which is the right one? If indeed there is a divine being responsible for the creation of humanity, why are there varied accounts of him in their religious texts?

The world is divided into two. There are some who believe in a creator of some kind and there are those who do not. Despite the copious research into the subject of creation, our origin as a species is still shrouded in mystery. What do we really know about our origins outside the mass of speculations and conjectures? Nothing. Sad to say we have achieved unimaginable feats yet we cannot answer the question of our origin. The reality is that we may never truly know the answer to that question in our generation. But our origin is not the only vexing question which torments us.

RELIGION

It is interesting to note that more than half the population on this earth believe in some kind of a deity and in this context I would refer to the deity as God. The reality is this; who is right? Is it the Christians, Muslims, Hindus, Buddhist? Each believes he or she is right. They all cannot be right and wrong at the same time. So how did this happen?

Is there indeed a supreme being sitting in the sky looking over us and judging us by our ways and even our thoughts? If indeed there is a supreme being, why are there so many variations of the same being? Did mankind use religion as a means to explain the unknowable? It could be but still it is curious that many of our problems in this world are partly to be blamed on religion.

Countless wars have been fought in the name of religion. Whole cities pillaged, women, children murdered because humanity wanted to declare their God supreme over another.

Is this what a supreme being would have wanted? This is the reality we are faced with. A religion where we do not question anything but believe in it just because we feel it is right. The moment you develop a conscience and you begin to question, you are labeled as a heretic. Is this the progress we want as a species? Is it right to let a child die because of religious faith? The rational answer would be no, but alas countless children have died because their parents or wardens had a certain kind of faith which prohibited blood from being exchanged. This is what religion does. A religion that subjugates women as the second best and always inferior to men. This is the reality we live in.

The same religion which provides comfort and provides us with a moral code is the same one used to murder innocents, cause racial segregation and stifle development. Why would any thinking being blow up himself to get some virgins in an eternal life? Ridiculous isn't it? Yet that is the reality. Humans would kill, maim, ridicule and do all sorts of horrendous things all in the name of religion. How did we get to this point as a species?

Countless generations have suffered misery all because of religion. While I must admit it would be disingenuous of me to credit all our problems to religion. I must say that religion has also done good in some parts of the world. Without religion where would be the objective basis of morality? But the reality is this; which religion is right?

There are many who posit that religion was used by the elites to enslave the masses. Maybe they are right. But there is no evidence to suggest such a deliberate attempt to beguile mankind in such a manner. Is religion then just a figment of our imagination? Maybe. But let's not put all the blame on religion, it has done good for this world at least. But from where I come from, it has not done much for us. Don't get me wrong, I have nothing against religion. But essentially I don't see much improvement in the lifestyle of people.

What essentially is the purpose of religion or believing in a supreme being? Some may scoff at the concept of religion or the idea of eternal bliss and damnation. But these ideas are not to be trifled with. Who are we to tell if it is wrong? What if there is a supreme being indeed? We do not have the luxury of fully knowing that answer in our present life. The origins of religion is shrouded in mystery like our beginning as a species and perhaps one day we might finally get to answer the question of religion. But before that we have the very reliability of our history to contend with.

HISTORY

History, a preserve of our ancient deeds and secrets. Our history chronicles humanity's achievements and failures in equal measure. But the reality is this, can we trust our history as a people? History is always rewritten by the conquerors. How do we really know if no agenda was embarked on to falsify records?

How do we know if notable events in our history are indeed true?

Many books have been written about the prehistoric age but apart from scientific analysis, how can we tell for sure that such historic facts are not simply just complicated lies. Even scientific facts have been proven to be lies.

Take for instance the history of our beginning. It is shrouded in mystery even to this day. Even the history of religion, the church especially is questionable. How can we tell if the version of history we are being told is simply a convenient truth?

Take Christianity for instance. Why are there are so many variations of the same religion? Why is the central figure in Christianity surrounded by such controversy? There are questions we do not have answers to.

Unfortunately historical books sometimes do not offer much. Yet history a testament of our past, it is supposed to guide us to our future. We are prevailed upon not to make the same mistakes our ancestors did. In reality, can we rely on human history? There've been countless times in our human history where the truth has been hidden. For the greater good, they said. The church on countless occasions tried to suppress scientific reasoning in favour of religion. That even raises further questions about the ulterior motives of the church.

What about the writers of our history? Did they have any altruistic motive on preserving the past or they harboured prejudices and biases of their own? Surely they did. They were human after all. Did they interpret the past through the lens of prejudices? We may never know.

There are details of our history as humanity which have been lost. What was in the great library of Alexandria? Where was Jesus Christ during his teenage years? Was Atlantis real or just a fictional city? These and many more are details of history we will never know. In fact, the reality would have been much worse if there was no written record at all. Better it be tainted than nothing at all. We can only hope that history has been good to us.

TECHNOLOGY

Sometimes the old ways are the best. I don't believe James Bond meant that. Gone were the days when humanity relied on good old manual labour to do stuff. But that time is gone. Technology in health, environment has seen the rapid acceleration in places hitherto would have been impossible. What would it be like in fifty years, a hundred years to come? I cannot begin to fathom the heights to which humanity would ascend to. I believe there will be breakthroughs in the fields of medicine. Robotics would make a giant stride. Most human functions would be done by robots.

But with the rise in technology we must also begin to question how far we are willing to go as humanity?

Would cloning of human beings be finally accepted? Many movies have tried to extrapolate the ramifications of such a technology on humans. What would be some of the ethical dilemmas in cloning?

Is too much technology bad? The advent of sex dolls or robot dolls if I may use the term is not something new. Would future technologies make them more lifelike and responsive to humans? It raises further ethical dilemmas for humanity with respect to how far we are willing to go. The reality is that the more we increase in bounds in technology it becomes a question of when and not why.

But the reality is this, with more technology comes an even greater responsibility to ensure that it is used for the greater good. But at what cost should such technologies be used? What cost would future generations bear for the technology of today?

Not only would cloning become possible but genetic manipulation may become a reality. Would humanity have the power to determine the sex of the child before it is born? These are the ethical questions to be answered with the technology of the future.

But with increasing technology, another danger looms on the horizon. The more technologically advanced we become, we also become more efficient at manufacturing weapons of mass destructions. Let's not kid ourselves. The future will not be one of just flying cars, longevity but is one where the threat of human extinction due to advanced weaponry would be more pronounced. Will the technology of the future be helpful? Only the future will tell but another reality also dawns.

SPACE EXPLORATION

If our ancestors had been shown a future where Neil Armstrong would land on the moon, they would have scoffed at such a ridiculous idea. But not only did he land on the moon but he walked on it. The reality of space exploration in the near future is that a part of humanity would dwell among the stars. This is not a prophecy but looking at the current state of technology, there can be no doubt about that.

But with space explorations comes an even deeper conundrum, how do we ensure it works? Who does the policing? No doubt treaties would have to be signed.

But the overriding question that anyone interested in space exploration has to confront is; is there really something out there?

It is interesting to note that despite living on this planet for years we are yet to discover any spark of intelligent life apart from us in the cosmos. It begs the question why earth is the only planet supporting life as we know it? Yet there are countless planets and galaxies out there. What is the purpose indeed?

But let's imagine for a moment we do find life out there. Oh! My! That would be something. It would change everything and I mean literally everything. But the reality is that we cannot afford to live on such imaginations. If there was life elsewhere, wouldn't we have found it by now?

Space exploration might not be the flashy ships and wormholes we see in Star Trek but it certainly would be an interesting time for mankind to live among the stars. But while we travel to live among the stars we must also look to earth where climate change is haunting us.

CLIMATE CHANGE

The reality is that climate change is a real phenomenon and not an abstract one like many people have been led to believe. With the polar caps melting, it is imperative that we take this issue seriously. I don't believe in extreme sentiments such as extinction to put fear into people without any scientific basis. Climate change is one thing we cannot run from. Can we do something about it? Yes. But let's not imagine for a moment that it's going to be an easy journey. People need to change their attitude. It's heartwarming to see teenagers such as Greta Thunberg on the forefront for climate change but it shouldn't end there. With rising sea levels, deforestations and rising carbon emissions, countries must be brought together to deal with this menace once and for all.

We might have the best technology but of what use would it be if future generations have to bear the brunt of our mistakes. Climate change action must start with us individually. It is a sad thing that some countries have turned a deaf ear to the issues on climate change but that shouldn't deter us from taking this fight. Posterity would not forgive us if we fail in this duty. The reality is if we do hope to have any future at all for our generation, then climate change would have to be tackled with all seriousness and commitment.

REALITY

Maybe we will finally put an end to climate change. Maybe we will finally conquer the stars. We are making technological advancements which some few years back would have been impossible but at what cost. We can only hope for the best the future brings. The future is still uncertain. Would we be able to answer the question of humanity's origins and purpose once and for all?

The truth is that at best we can come up with educated and plausible answers. One can only ask what is truly the purpose for humanity?

Is reality just a matter of living and dying and returning to the earth or is there something much more to this? When looking at the vastness of space, do you ever wonder where it all comes from? Is there a grand design to this life or just a random event? What happens when we die? Is the concept of an eternity just a crutch to satisfy our whims and imaginations? Is reality all that we see with our eyes or is there much more to this life?

The ultimate reality is that we may never know the answers to all the questions in this life. Perhaps generations after us would be able to finally put to rest these gnawing questions. The honest truth is that we only get to live once and we might as well enjoy this reality no matter how it is.

As Chuck Palahniuk in Diary said "We all die. The goal isn't to live forever, the goal is to create something that will."

This might be the only reality we've got and we better make damn sure we make the best use of it.

Don't miss out!

Visit the website below and you can sign up to receive emails whenever N.K. Aning publishes a new book. There's no charge and no obligation.

https://books2read.com/r/B-A-WWEE-LXNQB

BOOKS 2 READ

Connecting independent readers to independent writers.

Did you love *The Dilemma*? Then you should read *The Conjuring*[1] by N.K. Aning!

How far would you go to save your family?

Milton Freeman witnessed the tragic demise of his parents in a freak accident. He would have given anything to have them back. But now his younger brother, Josh is in a life threatening condition. He is the only family left.

He makes a deal to save his brother's life, but Milton is about to learn that some deals are better left alone.

Something beyond his imagination is coming for him. An evil that intends to take his soul if he lets it.

Read more at https://www.facebook.com/N-K-Aning-879564645456623/.

---

1. https://books2read.com/u/4XorQ6

2. https://books2read.com/u/4XorQ6

Also by N.K. Aning

Imaginaterium
Pierce and the City of Imaginaterium
Pierce and the Fallen Gods
The legend of Pierce and Peter : The Dawn

Poetry
In Her Eyes
The Agony of Life
A Memory of Death

Short Stories
The Bronze Man's Secret
Jack and God
Jason And The Great Dragon
The State
First Contact
The Agony of a Slave

Watch for more at https://www.facebook.com/N-K-Aning-879564645456623/.

About the Author

N.K. Aning is the author of more than seven books. His notable works include Prophecy, Damned, The Addiction, The Conjuring, Pierce and the City of Imaginaterium. He is a graduate from the University of Cape Coast in Ghana. He lives in Tema. He enjoys reading all things mystery, supernatural, fantasy and detective novels. N. K. Aning enjoys watching and reviewing some of his favourite movies.

Read more at https://www.facebook.com/N-K-Aning-879564645456623/.

Lightning Source UK Ltd.
Milton Keynes UK
UKHW010630300721
388036UK00001B/179